**BUDGERIGARS**
KW-011

# Contents:

Introduction—6
The Wild Budgerigar—10
Care and Breeding—28
Feeding–The Natural Way—56
Color Strains—68
Color Combinations—104
Non-Color Mutations—108
The Pet Budgerigar—110
The Sick Budgerigar—122
Index—125

**Photographers:** Dr. G. Allen, Dr. Herbert R. Axelrod, Walter Chandoah, Kerry V. Donnelly, Michael Gilroy, Keith Hindwood, Harry V. Lacey, Horst Mueller, Aaron Norman, L. Robinson, Schindel, Vincent Serbin, Louise van der Meid, Vogelpark Walsrode, Dr. M. Vriends, Wayne Wallace.

Distributed in the UNITED STATES by T.F.H. Publications, Inc., One T.F.H. Plaza, Neptune City, NJ 07753; in CANADA to the Pet Trade by H & L Pet Supplies Inc., 27 Kingston Crescent, Kitchener, Ontario N2B 2T6; Rolf C. Hagen Ltd., 3225 Sartelon Street, Montreal 382 Quebec; in CANADA to the Book Trade by Macmillan of Canada (A Division of Canada Publishing Corporation), 164 Commander Boulevard, Agincourt, Ontario M1S 3C7; in ENGLAND by T.F.H. Publications Limited, Cliveden House/Priors Way/Bray, Maidenhead, Berkshire SL6 2HP, England; in AUSTRALIA AND THE SOUTH PACIFIC by T.F.H. (Australia) Pty. Ltd., Box 149, Brookvale 2100 N.S.W., Australia; in NEW ZEALAND by Ross Haines & Son, Ltd., 18 Monmouth Street, Grey Lynn, Auckland 2, New Zealand; in SINGAPORE AND MALAYSIA by MPH Distributors (S) Pte., Ltd., 601 Sims Drive, #03/07/21, Singapore 1438; in the PHILIPPINES by Bio-Research, 5 Lippay Street, San Lorenzo Village, Makati Rizal; in SOUTH AFRICA by Multipet Pty. Ltd., 30 Turners Avenue, Durban 4001. Published by T.F.H. Publications, Inc. Manufactured in the United States of America by T.F.H. Publications, Inc.

# BUDGERIGARS

Georg A. Radtke

Budgerigars are available in many color varieties, all of which have been produced by breeders in small home aviaries. Young birds have striped foreheads, while mature birds have lost these stripes.

The beautiful budgerigar above is a good quality bird as judged by the standards of the various worldwide budgerigar society rules. It costs no more to feed and maintain than a lower quality bird. Get the best quality bird you can afford.

# Introduction

It was only 140 years ago that the Australian budgerigar made its way to Europe. Nevertheless, this little member of the parrot family, *Melopsittacus undulatus* to use its scientific name, has become the most loved personality; ready adaptability to change to new surroundings, and its ability to develop in a very short time (with the help of us humans) the most strikingly colorful palette of color and pattern mutations have all contributed equally to this popularity. The budgie has also become a most suitable subject for geneticists as well

A normal mauve budgerigar. This variety is not as popular as some others, such as the brilliant blues, but it is of great value to the color breeder. It can, therefore, command a good price from large commercial aviaries.

as for the hobbyist breeder. Also contributing to its popularity are the facts that this little bird is relatively easy to tame and is remarkably competent to imitate the human voice as well as other noises. There have been many volumes written about the budgie (parakeet to many American readers), ranging from strictly scientific discussions to mere conversations about this tame little pet. We would here like to take the opportunity to present the most important as well as the most interesting facts from each special area in a well-rounded picture, at the same time trying to avoid becoming boring to the reader and overburdening him with a number of obscure facts. Hopefully, forty years of my own experience with parakeets should prove helpful.

*A striking lutino budgie.*

A magnificent photograph of a wild budgerigar attending its nest in a hollowed out tree in Australia. The two birds at right are descendants of the budgerigars brought from Australia.

# The Wild Budgerigar

The main breeding grounds of the budgie are found in Western Australia, New South Wales, and Victoria. The birds live and breed there in large flocks that frequent eucalyptus groves. As they are generally cavity-breeders, they seek out holes in trees, particularly those in the decaying wood of the eucalyptus trees. Single pairs often breed in close proximity to each other, several in one tree, and even occupy the roots of the tree. The budgie is by nature a very social bird, so when bred in captivity it will breed best in colonies in aviaries, where several pairs can live together. In nature this serves to preserve the species, as the most prominent enemies of the budgie are predatory birds and tree snakes. If one of the birds spots such an enemy, he immediately warns his flock and thus mobilizes many eyes that scan the surroundings for any changes.

Budgerigars fly from these colonies into the vast dry grasslands to feed. They live mainly off grass seeds in their different states of ripeness and also raise their young on these seeds. Out in the Australian steppes, and even more on the few water courses on which all living things depend in the rather dry country of Australia, they fall prey to their enemies even more easily. This is one reason why budgerigars live in large flocks and, at the first sign of danger, tear away in a soaring flight into the open landscape. Their long, swallow-like wings are perfectly suited for this type of life, while their green and yellow plumage provides an excellent camouflage when the birds rest at noontime in the open, sundrenched crowns of the eucalyptus trees. The explanation for their often nervous and headstrong behavior and sudden nightly uproars, seemingly without reason, can be found in their former life in the wilderness. This also accounts for their senseless tearing away if they escape, when they storm out into an unknown world of roofs and chimneys from where they very seldom find their way home again. All these characteristics of

*Due to the many mutations in color and pattern, the budgie is one of the most variegated and beautiful of birds. The birds shown here are examples of the basic green budgie, a cobalt normal, a gray normal, and an opaline light green.*

behavior are innate to the wild budgie and have been preserved through almost 150 years of domestication.

Australia's climate is very peculiar. While it is very hot and dry in summer, it rains a lot in winter and, in the southern part of the country, is rather cold at times. This is why the budgerigar, which usually starts breeding at the end of the rainy season (during the Australian spring) when everything is green and in bloom, can take some warm as well as some cold days when living in the Northern Hemisphere. As a rule, budgerigars do not need

Budgerigars, unlike many other parrots, are grassland birds and are accustomed to eating from the floor of their cage. They love to perch, however, and perches of various thicknesses should be offered so their feet and toes may be exercised.

heated quarters, but the tame keet can get well accustomed to the heated room without any harm to the bird. (For variety, we'll occasionally use the nickname keet—the parakeet—instead of budgie—from budgerigar—in our discussions.)

The Island Continent is known for its rather wide range of climatic changes, and they are not always caused by its geography. While it may rain for years regularly and at specific times, precipitation might suddenly become greatly reduced or there might be none at all. On the other hand, there might be unexpected rain in regions of pronounced dryness. The rainy season might, in different regions, become unexpectedly prolonged or, for that matter, suddenly terminated. The budgerigar, a migratory bird, can easily adapt to these changing climatic conditions, but the length of success of its breeding season depends mainly on the location and the amount of precipitation in a specific region. This accounts for the fact that the

budgie might suddenly disappear from a territory where it had been breeding for years and form a new colony in an area where one expects it the least. Where there are suitable trees, a waterhole, and grass that promises seeds, keets will breed, independent of season, as long as the weather is favorable.

It is the female's job to secure a nesting place, very often possibly after hard and long flights with other female birds. The female gnaws and molds a nesting cavity, custom-made from its opening to the hollow of the nest proper. During this time the male will accompany her efforts with specific chirping sounds and will occasionally feed her from his crop.

Among our domesticated birds, the female will insist on gnawing on even a smooth nesting box made of hardwood. This goes back to her nest-preparing activities in the wild. It is also the reason why a female budgie given to flying around the room will occasionally damage furniture by gnawing on it. The female not only has

*Natural branches make excellent perches due to the variations in width one piece of wood may contain. However, one must be sure that the wood has never been treated with chemicals of any kind.*

One of the greatest pleasures of budgerigar keeping is the opportunity to breed them and, hopefully, to produce a new color variety. The economics of budgie breeding are such that many a bird lover was able to handsomely supplement his income by breeding a few birds every month. The youngsters shown above are about three weeks old. On the right is a view into a nest box with a parent and her ten-day-old babies.

an innate desire to gnaw, but also strong beak muscles that enable her to build a nesting hole and also provide an excellent tool for defense. If you don't believe this, try just once to grab an untamed female keet with your bare hands or have a tame little keet unexpectedly nip your ear-lobe!

The female budgie, in its natural habitat, lays five eggs. They are pure white, as are those of most cavity-breeders, in order to aid camouflage. The eggs hatch at about the time that the first grass seeds have ripened to a milky consistency that makes them most digestible to the young as well as the older birds. Eggs will be hatched continuously, and while the new chicks are still sitting in the nest hole, a new clutch of eggs is being laid. This will continue as long as there is enough seed for feeding. If there is a large amount of seed due to sustained rain, then there will be constant breeding, even to the point of exhaustion of the parents. If the food supply becomes suddenly exhausted, the parents will give up their eggs, regardless if it is the first or the second clutch, and migrate with their young to find new feeding

grounds. During these migrations, an often great number of birds will perish due to lack of food and water. This is why the species can only be maintained by extreme breeding activity during the times when food is available.

While in dry territories, the budgie may only find dried seeds from a previous season, seeds that have fallen to the ground and could not germinate due to lack of moisture. However, the keet can adapt to such a situation. As a bird of the grasslands, it has learned to scurry on the ground, where it attentively searches for seeds. Unless breeding, budgies can live for long periods without water. The morning dew hanging from plants provides sufficient water for the keet to drink and bathe in. Only the strong and healthy birds survive such a time of selection of the fittest.

Today's birds, although bred in captivity, show the same type of behavior established while their ancestors lived in their Australian homeland. They will be easier to understand if we keep this in mind. By changing environmental conditions in aviaries and breeding rooms and providing steady food and places to breed, as well as artificial warmth and light, one simulates a permanent spring season. Changes of climate therefore do not take place or are simply avoided. This is why budgies and other Australian birds in captivity may breed continuously until they are totally exhausted or even die, a fact unfortunately exploited by unscrupulous breeders out for a fast buck. That budgies molt irregularly and at all seasons also goes back to this.

Only during breeding season do budgies drink regularly, as they require more water in order to prepare a sort of mushy substance in the crop ("crop milk") for the young to feed on. Otherwise budgies may not drink for days at a time and also think very little of taking a full bath. However, they rub and roll in wet grass and leafy vegetables, displaying all the movements commonly used when

*Although budgies of today live happily in captivity, they still exhibit many behavioral traits established by their wild ancestors.*

bathing. Moist plants remind the budgie of natural dew and elicit typical budgerigar bathing behavior. For those birds that live in aviaries, a warm rainfall simulates the sudden Australian rains and makes them take an honest-to-goodness bath in that heavenly shower.

In spite of the fact that their seed cups are filled, budgerigars kept in aviaries with a natural floor prefer to scurry busily on the ground looking for seeds, preferably for those that have already germinated. They do that not because they "know" it is good for them, but because this is the way their ancestors in the Australian grasslands

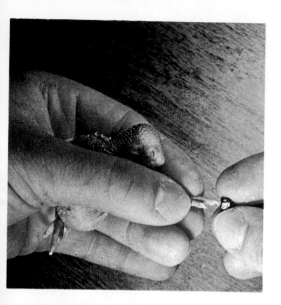

It is a good idea to band all parrots, including budgies, to prove that they were bred and were not taken from the wild. This practice is even required by law in some areas.

The birds below, almost one month old, are much too large to be banded. Banding assists the budgie breeder in keeping records on colors produced from different pairs.

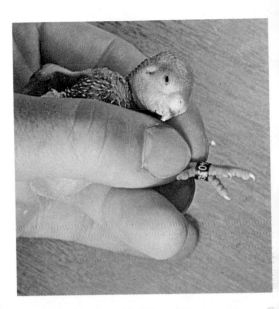

*The identifying band should be seamless and numbered. It is easily slipped on over the front tooo. The roar toe of the bird is then folded back. This process should take place when the bird is a few days old.*

Be sure to free the back toe after the band is slipped onto the chick's foot. There have been many cases where this little error has crippled a lovely budgerigar.

*One of the budgerigar's favorite toys is a swing, such as the one shown above. A variety of budgie toys is available at your pet shop.*

searched for their food. Even young, inexperienced keets who have only known dry millet seeds will immediately begin to pick from a half-ripened head of grass.

An exact description of the wild budgie is not necessary, as its markings are very similar to those of the green budgie sold in most pet shops. The wild bird, however, is smaller and slimmer. That they grow bigger when domesticated is a phenomenon common to many other animals. Shaw discovered and collected in 1800 the first grass-green "midget parakeet," and it was subsequently described in 1805. J. Gould first wrote about the bird in the wild and brought the first budgies to England in 1840, from where they victoriously invaded the rest of the world. Enormous importings at first only resulted in tremendous losses until it was finally learned how to care for these birds in the right way and how to breed them. In 1855 the Germans succeeded in breeding the birds. With the growing success of breeding in different European countries and later on also in the United States and Japan, the imports from Australia were first reduced and later, for the preservation of the species, completely forbidden by the Australian government.

While people were excited about the luminous green color of the wild budgie, their interest grew even more when the first color mutations began to appear in captive birds. That the budgie tends to produce such color mutations was already known by early observers of the wild Australian birds. Among thousands of light green birds can be found an occasional yellow, dark green, or opaline specimen.

*If one doesn't have enough time to spend with one's bird, a second should be kept. Two budgies will keep one another company and will prevent destructive habits, created by boredom, from forming.*

*All budgerigar colors can be traced back to the two basic colors: blue and yellow. If we take the yellow color from the normal light green (facing page, the bird in the nest box), we have a skyblue, which occurred as a separate mutation during the 1880s. The photo above shows a much admired color phase: the normal violet. The true, visible violet is a cobalt with the violet color added. When violet and mauve come together, the violet mauve comes into being. The yellow budgie is a lutino, the "albino" form of the blue-series birds.*

# Care and Breeding

If one wants to enjoy the natural behavior of a pair of budgerigars, one should select a large cage made of hardwoods or metal. A cage made from soft wood would soon be destroyed by the keet's natural tendency to gnaw. Only in a roomy cage will a single pair develop their full charm and elegance and even more so when they are regularly allowed to fly freely around the room. This exercise period should not exceed an hour or so, and the birds should only be let free under supervision so they do not get the idea that they may pick on furniture, wallpaper, or poisonous houseplants. Putting a treat into the cage will easily bring the birds back. It would be sufficient for the budgie to be allowed to fly just a few minutes around the room so that its flying muscles will remain fit.

As stimulation by companions is lacking for birds kept in captivity, the single pair, if not given a nest box, does not usually breed, though they will stick closely together and actively engage in playful wooing, the male trying to win the female. They also engage in preening each other's feathers (ornithologists term this social behavior), which can be noticed with many kinds of parrots as well as with finches. The male will bow many times in an engaging way before the female and finally feed her from his crop. While engaging in this sort of sexual play, their pupils contract to small dots.

Budgerigars enjoy their voices. They only become obtrusive and overly loud when partners are separated and cannot see each other, or if a bird alone in a cage feels lonely. The pitch of their voice when trying to locate each other sounds somewhat like that of the sparrow but is louder and more piercing. Its original function was to help a bird that had strayed find the flock in the Australian grasslands. There is also a loud cackling sound that signals excitement. This sound can even be produced by the young fledgling and in nature serves to warn or scare. The domesticated birds still have all these sounds at their disposal and use them, just as they use the

*A pied male and opaline female breeding pair preparing their nest box.*

The body color of the original budgerigar imported from Australia is light green with a yellow mask and black and yellowish shell-like markings on the wings. Fabulous prices were paid for new colors as long as they remained scarce. Today we have a wide spectrum of colors. In addition, birds with a small crest (right) may be bred in three different forms and with several variations within these forms.

mating call, in the constant chattering and twittering sounds of their courtship. A large flock of budgerigars kept in an aviary might amuse themselves for hours by communicating among each other with constantly changing sounds of whistling, twittering, and screeching, not always exactly soothing to one's nerves. This is why it might be wise for a prospective breeder to find out first how his neighbors feel about these noises. It will save a lot of irritation later, as in every fight about animals it is the animal that suffers most. The different sounds of a single pair of parakeets, by the way, seem to have more of a relaxing effect than a disturbing one.

The budgie's cage should be placed at eye-level in a bright area of a room that is free from drafts and not exposed to sunlight all day. Kitchen odors, tobacco smoke, and drafts are poison for our feathered pets and shorten their lifespan. The cage also should not be placed close to a heater or the T.V. Food and fresh drinking water must be available around the clock; water for bathing, however, is not necessary. The keet hulls its seed, discarding the empty hull into the feed cup. These hulls collect in the cup, so that the keet often cannot find the actual seed underneath. One should blow away the hulls at least twice a day. The budgie's metabolism works in such a way that it could literally die if it does not feed for 24 hours. In other words, if a bird does not eat for a day, it will be dead by next morning. If left in an overheated dry room, budgies tend to lose some of their feathers. While this does not actually constitute molting, it certainly impairs their looks and might become troublesome to the lady of the house. A room with moderate temperatures and sufficient humidity is healthiest for man as well as for the birds.

At times the claws and beak grow overly long, as they are not being used sufficiently in a cage. This hinders not only feeding, but also movements. Claws and beak will have to be trimmed with sharp scissors, but be

*If you plan to keep two or more budgies together, be sure there is ample room in the cage for each bird. In addition, be sure that there are enough perches to go around.*

careful to avoid injury to the fine blood vessels they contain.

Budgerigars usually do not suffer from parasites, but keeping the cage clean and changing the bottom sand should be routine

nevertheless. If you habitually stay up very late during the evenings, cover the cage. Lack of sleep in keets results in featherpulling and other nervous disorders. One should also guard against placing a cage in a picture window if it is not shaded with curtains. If your bird flies freely around the room, it will often not be able to distinguish an uncovered window pane. In attempting to fly through the glass a collision will result, with broken wings or a broken neck the probable result. Windows of bird houses should for that reason be covered with chicken wire in order to avoid a problem.

Some budgerigars are reported to have lived up to 20 years, but they were exceptional. A bird in captivity lives approximately seven to nine years, during six of which it may be bred. An unbred budgie might live to be 12 or 14 years if one raises it according to the suggested rules.

Breeding a pair of budgies in your living room does not make much sense, as you often have to be patient for many months before the birds will start to breed, which causes more trouble than pleasure. The beginner should start out with at least two pairs of birds so that he may avoid some disappointment. With two

pairs, the birds will stimulate each other's behavior and it will be much easier for them to start to breed. Not every pair is suitable for breeding.

Damp, dimly lit basement rooms or drafty attics that are hot in summer are unsuitable for breeding budgerigars. Ideally suited is a well-built aviary with a flight facing southeast or south in a draft-free location in the backyard or garden. It is, however, also possible to breed in sunny rooms or in a ground-floor room with an adjoining small flight linked to the birdroom by a window. There are no limits to your technical ingenuity, as the end justifies the means. We don't have room here to describe in detail different ways of building aviaries that are in use today, but this is covered in *Building an Aviary* by Naether and Vriends (T.F.H.). I would like to mention some ground rules, however, pertaining to materials and methods of construction.

Budgies may be bred in colonies, as was commonly done in the past, as well as in single breeding pairs, which is preferable today. With both

*When planning which birds to mate, be sure to take genetic traits, behavioral idiosyncrasies, and previous nesting habits into consideration.*

systems a roomy shelter and spacious flight are required. Before building a breeding facility, one would be well advised to take all this into account, especially with regard to available materials and money. With two single pairs you could still start breeding in a living room and provide a smaller cage for the chicks, but if you want to breed more than two single pairs, it is advisable to plan very carefully for it.

Cement, stone, or steel provides draft-free but damp and hard to heat rooms, while houses built from wood tend to get very hot in summer and are hard to keep free of parasites; additionally, rats or mice could enter wooden buildings below the ground. The best compromise is a foundation built of cement, with walls and roof built of sheets of plywood or particle board. It is also advisable to insulate the walls as well as the roof in colder climates. Large windows are necessary, and it is preferable to have skylights, but not too many, as too much heat and direct sunlight are not good for budgies. To accommodate the keet's liking for a fast flight, indoor aviaries as well as the flight should be connected by windows or doors that can be closed when not in use. These flights should be as long as possible, but should be narrow and not more than two meters in height. It is important that indoor aviaries and outdoor flights be easily accessible. To prevent escapes, a double door should be installed. Single or double breeding cages in blocks of four or six, according to available space,

may be installed on shelves up to four layers high, one on top of the other. Their construction should take into consideration that as much daylight as possible should reach the front of the breeding cages.

Modern large aviaries are usually built with inside housing and adjoining flights on one side; on the other side there are multiple-story breeding cages in blocks and a walkway sufficiently wide to allow easy access for feeding. If you want to save money, chicken wire could be used to close off the front of the breeding cages. More practical, however, are special wire screens which cannot injure the budgies' wings while they climb around on the wire. As birds need large amounts of oxygen, it is mandatory to provide good ventilation. Heat is only needed if one breeds in winter. A small heater or oil-stove is sufficient, as temperatures about 14° C. (58° F.) in winter are best for budgies.

In outside aviaries, a framework of iron pipes of different diameters covered

When budgerigars become ready to mate, their ceres change color. The female's cere darkens, while the male's turns bright blue.

with chicken wire and painted black has proven to be best. The black paint, in addition to providing protection for flying birds, also makes a good background for the colorful birds. One should erect this frame on a solid foundation of cement, which can easily be kept clean and prevent illnesses caused by dirt or spoiled food. Budgerigars prefer a sand or gravel floor over the cement. If you decide against a cement foundation, it will be necessary to bury chicken wire in a trench at least 30 cm (12 inches) into the ground to guard against mice. No tree branches of any kind should be on top of the aviary, as their movements in the wind could prove scary to the budgies. They might also provide easy access to pests.

Economical fluorescent bulbs in different sizes can provide the right light for a bird house when used in connection with incandescent bulbs of low wattage to provide the illusion of twilight. There are also inexpensive timers that can be easily regulated. They should switch on the bulbs of lower wattage first, then the fluorescent lights or vice versa. This simulates natural dawn and dusk, especially important for the females, which must not be surprised outside the nest box by sudden lighting changes. The birds will easily adjust to this lighting and, as soon as the bulbs of lower wattage are turned on, will seek out their nest boxes. In aviaries that are frequently subjected to outside disturbances such as street noises or searchlights, inexpensive nightlights should be left burning during the night. Even if you are not trying to breed birds, this might be advisable.

Colony breeding (keeping several pairs of breeding birds in the same aviary) can have the best results with the least amount of work, provided one sticks to a few ground rules. One breeding pair should be given at least one square meter of space, and more would be even better. The breeding cages should be uniform and should be suspended in the upper third of the aviary in such a manner that the light falls on

*A colony of blue-series birds.*

the nest box opening. Use upright nest boxes that have the entrance hole in the upper third of the box, with the nest proper directly underneath. Another type of nest box is rectangular, with the entrance hole on one side and the nest on the other.

There are advantages and disadvantages with both kinds of boxes. The upright nest boxes can be entered by the breeding birds directly so that they land directly upon the eggs, possibly damaging both eggs and chicks. In the rectangular boxes that have the entrance hole on the side, the female enters and moves sideways to the eggs. The rectangular nesting box safeguards the eggs as well as the chicks somewhat better against danger from the outside and prevents them from falling out or leaving the nest too early. You might want to compromise when using the upright box and provide a perch, a dowel inserted into a hole drilled into the wall of the nest box, so the female when entering may rest on this perch before lowering herself carefully onto the eggs.

Good measurements for nest boxes for budgies are 25 cm (10 inches) in height, 17x17 cm (7x7 inches) of floor space, and an entrance hole of approximately 4.5 cm (1⅘ inches) in diameter. Commercially available nest boxes are very often too small or their hollowed out nest cavity is too shallow. It is best to build one yourself, carefully avoiding seams and gaps, so that mites will not settle there. It is also advisable to have the floor scooped out sufficiently deep so that the eggs cannot roll into the corners of the nest box, thus preventing them from being well covered.

Naturally, one should only leave well selected breeding pairs together in the breeding cage. Do not leave extra single males or females with the breeding pair. Unattached males disrupt the complicated courting behavior of the budgie pairs, and single females sooner or later fight with their breeding rivals. While fights between males remain relatively harmless, female rivals will fight each other until one has been killed and the clutch of eggs will always be destroyed. Extra females have been seen moving from nest box to nest box, throwing eggs out of the nests of their rivals or killing their young. If this would happen to a novice breeder, it would certainly dampen or destroy his enthusiasm for further breeding.

Breeding pairs do not always remain "true" to each other, and the male is especially likely to be "unfaithful" when the female is sitting on the nest. If you are breeding in colonies but would like to have pure-bred birds, keep a pre-mating pair together in a single breeding cage so they become attached to each other. These

A pair of budgies in a temporary cage. When breeding budgies, be sure that there is ample room for each pair and that unattached birds cannot gain access to any nest boxes.

temporary boxes could be very simply constructed, as they are only meant to be used for a short period of time. In this manner one can avoid mating of birds that were not selected for pairing.

Keeping birds in communal aviaries will not only provide much pleasure and amusement from watching the birds' antics in a constantly changing picture, but will also give you the advantage of simplified feeding and cleaning. You could use several large feeders or hang up automatic feeding devices that are commercially available in many sizes. Instead of a standard seed mixture you might use a particular variety of seed, which is not only more economical but provides for the timid bird getting its fill. Seed mixed with cod-liver oil, however, cannot be used in automatic feeders. You will also need separate feeding cups for soft food.

Nesting boxes, especially when they are in aviaries, should be inspected daily. Budgerigars seldom object to this. If you do not want to endanger breeding, broken eggs or dead young must be removed immediately. It is a good idea to attach note pads to the outside of the breeding cages. On these you can enter all necessary notes on a specific clutch and on the success of a specific breeding pair and their peculiarities. It is safer to take the young away from their parents as soon as they can shift for themselves, which is at the age of approximately six weeks, and house them in separate cages, as they tend to disturb later mating attempts of the parent birds. The parent birds will often persecute offspring who try to enter their nest box, which they have been observed doing at a very early age.

A pair that has already bred two or three times should be separated so that one does not unduly weaken the birds. This forced separation is something that many cock birds object to, but it is necessary, especially as we in the Northern Hemisphere do not have the dry season of Australia to naturally interrupt breeding. Regardless of when one separates a breeding pair, there will always be eggs or chicks in a nest box, so it is a good idea to separate a pair immediately after they have finished breeding. There then should be only two or three fresh eggs in the nesting box.

Eggs or chicks of an especially valuable pair may be left for another breeding pair to care for. Most pairs, as they do not all start breeding at the same time, will have chicks of different clutches in their nest boxes at all times. Birds that have already bred and are now resting should be kept in large aviaries without nest boxes, the females and males separated. It is best, whenever possible, to keep the sexes separated by an aviary with young birds in between, otherwise the newly separated birds will cling to

*An opaline budgerigar. Breeders would suggest that this bird be mated to a budgie with a clear mantle, since this specimen has too much undulation in his shoulder area.*

the wire of the walls for days and not get any rest. If there is not enough room for such a separation, however, pairs can be kept together, but the nest box will definitely have to be removed at that time.

Neither temperature, amount of daylight, nor courting procedure of her partner stimulates the ovaries of the female budgie, but the presence of the nest box and certain types of foods do. Once again we see a definite parallel to the birds living in the Australian wilderness which have now adapted to new surroundings. While the birds cannot be deprived of food, we can, however, eliminate the type of food that would stimulate sexual activity. If this is done at the same time the nest box is removed, it will prompt regression of the sexual organs in the female as well as in the male, thus promoting a resting period. Breeders specializing in pure-bred birds have left male and female birds together when they are not breeding by using this technique. More than that, one has found that the resting birds, when left together, will gain less weight as they remain more active. As this results in more successful future broods, this method is advisable.

Breeding in separate cages is mandatory if one wants to breed specific colors, as proof of parentage is necessary. This separate breeding cage method is also used more and more by breeders specializing in particularly tame birds that are best suited to talking. Breeding in single cages requires more work and is less natural, but it also has

some advantages, such as preventing fights between rival males as might occur in an aviary.

The smallest breeding cage should be 50 cm (20 inches) long, preferably more. Double breeding cages, in as many stories as desired, can be put on top of each other if desired. This would also make it possible to affix the breeding cages in the upper third of the aviary, which is not only practical but also saves room. The birds have more room, and the breeder has the added advantage of being able to control the breeding cages from the outside. One could also use shelves with breeding cages, placing the cages next to each other to save room. The nest boxes would then have to be attached to the front, either on the outside or inside, of the breeding cage. Attaching them to the inside would make it too difficult to control the nest boxes, while hanging them on the front bars of the cage would deprive them of light. Some pairs breed less successfully if the entrance hole is on the opposite side from where the

*Each of these pretty birds has a show fault that would damage its chances in competition. To avoid propagating such faults, try to breed birds whose strong points will balance with each other's weak points.*

keeper approaches. In order to facilitate care and make it easier to observe, and also to provide circulation of air and regulate humidity, leave a space between the top shelf and the roof and between the bottom shelf and the floor.

To make cleaning the cages easier, a sliding bottom drawer that is not too shallow is important. Cover the floor of the cage with medium fine sand that has been washed or with several layers of butcher's paper. The paper is removed daily, layer by layer, with the least possible disturbance to the birds. Regardless of the method used, the floor must remain dry and clean at all times.

Breeding cages can be made of almost any wood, and even a good grade of exterior plywood is satisfactory. Two perches are sufficient for each breeding cage. They should be solidly affixed to the cage wall at approximately half the height of the cage so that the birds will not damage their wing feathers on the bars of the cage. These two perches should also be far enough apart from each other that the birds will have to hop—or, even better, fly—when moving from one to the other. They should be made out of hardwood with a large enough diameter and a rough surface so the budgies can get a good grip on them, especially during mating. Oval or square perches have also been used successfully. Water can be kept in little water cups next to the perches. Plastic cups are easy to care for, and additives like vitamins are preserved longer in them. Seed cups should be made out of glass or glazed ceramic, as light cups might be easily tipped over by the playful birds. There are a variety of commercial cups that can be inserted through the cage wires to hold grit and cuttlebone (for calcium).

We do not recommend automatic feeding devices. Mixed seed is often thrown out of the seed cup by the budgies and is therefore not economical. Also, some mixed seed may lead to constipation. It would not only be a great loss to have breeding birds die of hunger, but it would also be very cruel.

As already mentioned, budgerigars can be bred at any time of the year. Some commercial breeders breed all year round, taking turns with different breeding pairs; others use one group of paired birds in spring and another in fall. It is best to follow the experience of other breeders in your area. In any case, birds bred in winter need a mildly heated building. The best time for breeding is spring, as fresh green food is available.

When breeding in colonies in aviaries, breeding pairs should be started at the same time to avoid fighting with new additions. When breeding in single cages, one should wait for a pair to be sexually ready before putting them in together. This readiness might be verified by checking the birds' ceres (area around the nostrils). The cock's cere will be smooth and of a bright, shiny, deep blue; the hen's cere will be deep brown. One should never breed birds that are in full molt. They should also have displayed their typical courting behavior: while the male performs a little dance, nodding his head and his pupils contracted in sexual excitement, the female picks on everything in sight, and both birds feed each other. It is wise to put the female, who is at that time highly nervous, into the breeding cage a few days earlier so that she will have time to acclimate herself

*Never allow your budgie to fly outdoors without some sort of restraint. Budgies will undoubtedly fly away from their owner in such a situation, and may thus be lost forever.*

to the new surroundings. She will also lose a little of the weight accumulated during the resting period. Budgies used to companions will eat only a little when put in a cage by themselves, which is of advantage in this case. The female is then especially willing to accept the male selected for her by the breeder, even if she has already been attached to an unsuitable male in the aviary.

Provide a nest box only after the new pair has become strongly attached to each other. Otherwise, the female might disappear into the box and not reappear often enough for the male to complete mating, which is a rather laborious process with budgies. This would result in unfertilized eggs. Not every breeder will have sufficient time to observe the birds, but if definite mating behavior has been observed, then one should select a time when the male is feeding his mate to put the nest box into the breeding cage.

If the hen has bred previously, you can expect the first egg to be laid in approximately eight days, but young females might take up to three weeks, so don't be impatient. Only if the hen does not lay any eggs within four to six weeks is it safe to presume that she is either ill or infertile. Occasionally there might be a genetic malformation of the oviduct, a degenerative defect developed during the course of domestication. When this happens the eggs become lodged in the abdomen, where they are resorbed. It also sometimes happens that the cock is sterile.

If everything runs its normal course, the female will lay an egg every two days until a maximum clutch of nine eggs has been laid. The young female, however, may produce as few as three to five eggs. The hen will then remain steadily in the nest box after the first egg is laid, so the first clutch of eggs will be hatched within 18 days. The chicks are hatched about two days apart from each other. It is almost a little miracle that the female, even in the complete darkness of the nest box, cares for her chicks of different sizes and ages individually, but not even the youngest fledgling will be forgotten. At hatching the last chick is smaller than the foot of its 15-day old brother or sister, but it will be as well fed as the others. It is advisable, however, to take the young from such a large clutch and distribute them to other nest boxes with fewer chicks, so that one female has no more than five young to care for at a time. Up to the age of three weeks, chicks will be easily accepted by their adoptive parents.

During their first days, the chicks are fed primarily by the hen with a secretion rich in protein which she regurgitates to feed her chicks. This secretion is produced in the proventriculus, in contrast to pigeons, which prepare the secretion in their crops. As the young grow older this secretion will be mixed with predigested food that has first been eaten by the cock, who transfers it to the female, who in turn feeds it to the

*Nest areas, in addition to everyday cages, should also be provided with perches.*

chicks. When the chicks are 14 days old, the male will start to participate in direct feeding. After 30 to 35 days, when the young start to fly, the male will completely take over the feeding.

When young budgies leave their nest box, they are fully feathered and equipped to fly, but for a few days they are still helpless but will rapidly start to feed. After 14 days, at the most, they are fully self-supporting. Some hens that have started a new clutch after their young leave the nest become very aggressive against their young, biting and injuring them dangerously. This is why it is advisable to separate the young birds from their parents within two to three days and put them into a small cage with a feeding cup directly in front of them. Most of the birds will adapt easily, and the younger ones are often fed by their older brothers and sisters. One might also put older, unattached males with them in the same cage, and they will take over the feeding. This way you can eliminate a lot of losses.

Young budgerigars show dull colors and incomplete markings. Their eyes are uniformly dark and without the light sclerotic ring of the older bird. The cere of young male birds is mostly pink, while that of the female is, strangely enough, of a bluish color, which easily leads to a wrong diagnosis when determining a bird's sex too early. The typical coloration of the waxy cere develops slowly. The budgie is not mature until nine months old, and only at that time does it reach its final coloration. For that reason a keet should not be bred too early. It is absolutely necessary that the keeper let a bird enjoy the aviary, where it can fly freely, enjoy sunlight and fresh air, and take showers in the warm summer rain before it is bred. This is especially important for a bird that is to be bred in a single breeding cage.

Interrupting breeding in a single breeding cage is simple. As soon as the last young keet from the second clutch has left the nest, remove the hen, the nest box, and also the third clutch that might already have been started. The male will then take over the feeding of the young until such time as all of the birds can be transferred from their breeding cages to aviaries. This is the time to thoroughly clean the breeding cages, nest boxes, and all other breeding equipment. It is advisable to place the females in a cage located far enough away so they cannot hear the males. If they hear or see each other, they will stay in contact and a real resting period will not be guaranteed. After the separation the female will often lay one or two more eggs, which should be discarded. The female will be quite sensitive to cold and drafts for a while and should not be exposed in an outside aviary, especially during winter.

Three clutches might be justified when the eggs of a previous clutch have been unsuccessful due to the fact that they were infertile (clear) or the young died. By the way, it is not the production of eggs for breeding itself that is strenuous for a breeding pair, but the rearing of the chicks. After the eggs

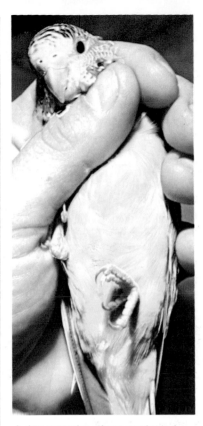

*A demonstration of one method of holding a budgie.*

have been incubated for approximately eight days, one can recognize fertile eggs by holding them against a bright light (such as a strong flashlight). Fertilized eggs look reddish because of the blood vessels; a spoiled egg shows an air bubble on its round end and is otherwise completely dark. Unfertilized eggs remain clear and transparent. If one discovers this way a whole clutch that has not been fertilized, it might be wise to put one to three chicks into the nest so as not to interrupt the natural rhythm of breeding. Experience has shown that fertilization of the following clutch is usually helped by having the birds raise their adopted young; simply removing the clear eggs just speeds up the time to the laying of the next batch of eggs.

Until their eighth day, budgie chicks are naked and blind. The underdown appears first and, depending on the final coloring of the bird, is either white or gray. Next the wing feathers and then the tail feathers grow; beginning at approximately the fourteenth day, the colorful contour feathers will appear.

The birds may be banded with a closed ring before leaving the nest box. Closed rings are necessary if you wish to show your birds or if you want to keep an exact record of their inheritance. When the chick is six to nine days old, take it in one hand and grab its leg in such a manner that the three front toes are extended next to each other. With your free hand slip the ring over the toes and the joint. Finally, using a blunt wooden stick, slip the fourth toe through the ring. If banded too early, the ring will slip off the chick. If banding is done a little late, a drop of oil or saliva will help slip the band on without injuring the keet. Immediately jot down the number of the bird's band on the card that you have attached to the breeding cage. This is important so that you will have a record of the bird's ancestry when it is moved from one nest to the other.

There might be an occasional accident during the breeding season. The hen might neglect feeding her chicks sufficiently or even engage in feather-plucking. In either case, the chicks must be immediately removed and placed into another nest box. Young females might not feed their chicks well because their proventriculus does not produce enough milk. If this is the case, the first batch of chicks will die but a later one

*A lutino budgie being banded. Banding and accurate record keeping will make the breeder's task much easier when future matings are planned.*

would be well cared for.

The droppings of healthy chicks are solid and dry quickly. It is, nevertheless, advisable to put a handful of sawdust into the nest proper. You will, however, find that some hens will remove this by pushing it out of the nest. Don't worry too much about this but be sure to clean the nest box after the breeding is completed. Some breeding pairs feed their young too many wet substances. This is not necessarily unhealthy, but be careful that the feet and beaks of the young chicks do not become encrusted. If these crusts are not removed regularly, malformations are possible during this stage of quick growth. One frequently sees budgies whose upper beaks have grown into their lower beaks; this may well be a sign of genetic degeneration.

Always remembering important aspects such as color and genetic make-up, it is recommended that you pair an older, experienced cock with a young female or a young male with an experienced female. This way quality as well as quantity improves, as it is possible to avoid losses caused by the inexperienced young bird, either male or female, and prevent establishment of bad habits that are hard to correct. Some young cocks will push themselves on the females, even to following them into the nest boxes, which easily causes breakage of eggs. The birds will in this case try to push the broken eggs out of the nest box, getting themselves soiled with the sticky contents of the egg. When cleaning themselves off afterwards they might develop a taste for eggs. This is how many a notorious egg-eater—male or female—was born. At times it is possible to correct such behavior by putting artificial plaster or ceramic eggs (sold for this purpose in pet stores) into the nest. After trying to hack into this granite-like material, they often lose their desire to pick at other eggs.

At the other extreme are breeding pairs that sit for hours peacefully next to each other in the nest box. There are even cock birds that will, together with the hen, engage in hatching the eggs. These cocks very often make the best fathers, who will immediately help in feeding and caring for the chicks. A male of such qualities can be left to raise the chicks should the female, for some reason or other, become incapacitated. Should something happen to the male, the female will take over and raise up to four chicks on her own. In any such case, one should not give such a female a new male, as she would either leave her chicks and mate anew or, more infrequently, kill the new male. Fighting female budgies immediately aim for the head of the male and can pierce the skull with only a few bites. They will fight in this way only when they are defending their nests. If the female kills a new male, she does so because she considers him to be an intruder.

We have already talked about the bad habit of feather-plucking, done mostly

*Headstudy of a color mosaic hen.*

by females and to a lesser degree by males. Lightly plucked chicks will soon grow new feathers, but if the plucked chicks are not immediately removed from the female, she will pluck off all the babies' feathers. It takes months for chicks damaged in such a way to recuperate, if at all. Why parrots pluck their young while they are still feeding them (not only budgies engage in this bad habit) is not fully known. At first the mother playfully pulls her chicks' growing quills—

through which blood passes during the development of the feather—through her beak. Biting into one of the quills might give the hen a taste for blood. Some females pluck only the first down and leave the contour feather intact. That will not have any permanent ill effects, as down will grow again. There is one school that maintains that the female plucks her chicks' feathers because she lacks minerals; this could be prevented by a balanced diet for the breeding female.

Seeds of different grasses provide the basic food for the wild budgerigar. Looked at botanically, millet, canary seed, and oats are nothing but cultivated grasses, which explains why this type of food is most easily accepted and digested. Today these are the basic foods of our domesticated birds. There are many kinds of millet and canary seed, and they are grown in many different areas. In pet stores you might purchase well balanced mixtures of all of these, but there are seeds that are more pleasing to the human eye than to the bird's digestion. Hard-hulled Dakota millet from the USA, for example, will be rejected by the bird and is often hard to digest. Golden millet, imported from Morocco, is also much better looking than it is good, especially for young budgies, as it is too hard. On the other hand, gray and unattractive millet imported from Japan is of excellent quality but seldom imported, as is mohair millet imported from India.

Commercial budgie food contains La Plata millet, which is pale yellow, of medium size, and not especially attractive, but fortunately very good for the birds. The same can be said about the white proso millet that has large kernels and comes from the USA. It is not extremely nourishing, but it is soft. There is also a dull yellow, small millet from Senegal that is contained in some of the mixtures. The birds like it, and it is well suited for the young. Good quantities of canary seed from Morocco should be added to each mixture of budgie seed. The long yellow kernels with a brown core are easily digestible, rich in nutrients, and easily hulled. This is why they are the first seeds that the young birds will accept when they start to feed on their own. Breeders in England feed mixtures that contain a maximum of 30% canary seed. Commercial mixtures also contain 2-5% hulled oats; this is just right for pet birds, as an overabundance of oats will make the bird gain too much weight.

For the breeder who has more than two breeding

*In order to have healthy, happy budgies, one must be sure to provide a nutritious and interesting diet for one's birds.*

pairs, I would advise buying different seeds in bulk. These could be used in automatic feeding devices in the aviaries or mixed according to the individual needs of the birds. The advantage of mixing your own seeds is that the mixture can be changed according to different needs during the time of breeding, raising chicks, and the resting time of the grown budgies. During breeding the birds should be fed a mixture of at least 40% of the best canary seed and 10% of one or more of the millets. For the resting bird there should be a mixture of 30% canary seed, 35% Plata millet, and 35% proso millet. These numbers are only meant as guidelines and should be modified as you gain experience. Some breeders feed niger seed, lettuce seed, or linseed, all of which contain a lot more fat than the grasses, which consist mainly of carbohydrates (starches). Small quantities of oil seeds are also good for the budgie that is accustomed to them, as they stimulate growth of feathers and enhance their glow.

Hulled oats are not required in a mixture during breeding time, and as a matter of fact they are not even good for the birds. We recommend that you buy whole, well cleaned feed oats directly from a farmer or feed store. As it has especially large hulls, one would have to offer it in special feeding cups, which has the advantage that you can measure them according to the birds' needs. Oats are the one major seed among the grains that contain protein and other important nutrients, including minerals. If budgerigars are kept in cool rooms, they may be fed as much oats as they like during the winter. During summer it should not be fed exclusively so that the birds do not grow too fat. During breeding season it should first be germinated and then fed to the birds. Budgies will quickly learn to husk whole kernels of oats, and thus their upper beaks will become worn down in a natural way. Most of the nutrients are contained right under the outer hull.

To germinate oats, simply

*A yellowfaced skyblue and a banded Australian pied skyblue.*

pour whole kernels of oats into large flat trays. Cover these with water and let them stand in a warm place for 24 hours. Then drain the water, rinse the oats in a large sieve under running water, and let them stand for another 24 hours in a warm place. The small white sprouts at the end of the large expanded kernels are just right to be used for feeding. You will have to prepare a daily supply of approximately one tablespoon per pair. Remove left-overs from the cups daily and wash the cups thoroughly with hot water, as left-overs will turn sour.

Canary seed and millet can be germinated in the same way, preferably separately. Quickest to germinate are Senegal millet and Plata millet; different types of canary seeds take longer. If at all possible and if there is time and room to do so, feed as much sprouted seed as possible during breeding season and also during the time when the young are growing. This natural food will give you excellent results.

Budgerigars living in freedom feed on dry and fully ripened kernels only at the end of their breeding season and during migration. Before that, they feed on grasses in all stages of ripeness, beginning with the blossoms and half-ripened seeds. For this reason it is best to supplement their regular food with half-ripened seeds and grasses. It would also help to save on seed costs. Oats and wheat can be found from June until fall and blue grasses (Poa) may even be found in the middle of winter under bushes and in gardens. You will have to use trial and error to find out which of the local grasses and weeds are liked best by your budgerigars. It is important that these foods be fresh and picked only in fields that have not been treated with chemicals. Small bundles of weeds are pushed between the wires of the breeding cages. Large bundles might also be hung in aviaries, where it is a delightful experience to see a flock of colorful budgies gather around them.

The best wild green food for budgies in spring and fall is chickweed (Stellaria media), especially its buds and seed pods. In regions where there is little snow, chickweed can be found all year round. If there is not too much of it, the birds will also eat their leaves and stems. One should take care not to feed it when frozen or withered. It can be found in gardens, on compost heaps, in fields and in orchards. Chickweed is a spreading low weed hated by both the farmer and the gardener, so be especially careful, as many of the areas where it grows have been treated with weed-killers deadly to birds.

Lettuce, spinach, dandelion leaves, and a number of seeding meadow grasses, provided the birds will eat them, are also suitable for budgies and good for their health. Apples and other fresh fruit, as well as chopped or ground carrots, are good substitutes for greens in winter. Unfortunately, the budgie, more than other birds, is quite conservative where food is concerned: it mistrusts any new food it is not familiar with. Many pet budgies die because their owners are not aware of this and will offer "new" foods only once. A budgie may panic on seeing an orange carrot or a dangling green lettuce leaf for the first time, but it will finally try them if fresh food is patiently offered over a matter of days and weeks. Adjusting birds to new foods is easier in aviaries, where there are many birds. The noisiest, most daring, bird—who is often the leader—will try anything new first, and the others will follow. Budgerigars used to different kinds of greens will invariably feed their young on these, too. Even after a chick's first two or three days, one can often see green particles in the pre-digested food in the chick's transparent crop.

Fresh, preferably budding twigs of willow, poplar, and fruit trees will provide good food supplements during the winter. They fill the budgie's need to gnaw and pick and at the same time provide nutrients of many kinds contained under the bark, in the tree sap, and especially in the bud.

Spray millet should also be mentioned. These sprays (seed heads) are approximately 10-30 cm (4-12

*If one keeps several budgies, there is usually one who is bolder than the rest—one who will try new foods and persuade his companions to do the same.*

inches) long and rather expensive. However, this is a worthwhile expense. Millet sprays are readily accepted by practically all granivorous birds, especially parrots and exotic finches. They are also preferred by very young birds and sick and old ones. This is easily explained. As soon as the seed has ripened, the germ enclosed in the seed coat has already begun the slow process of dying, the duration of which is entirely dependent on the time spent in storage. The seed can only be reactivated by producing a new plant when it comes in contact with humidity. The fresher it is and the more vitality it still contains, the quicker it will germinate. Experienced breeders take a sample when buying seed. If a millet spray is left in water, the seeds should start sprouting within 24 hours. As long as the seeds remain in their panicles on the head linked to the mother plant, even if that is already dead, they will die more slowly than seeds that have been harvested and stored separately. That is the whole secret of spray millet, which,

except for its origin, is not much different from Senegal millet.

If you are a gardener, you might plant your own millet, taking care to select a type of millet that is not too susceptible to disease and best suited to the climate in your specific area; follow specific directions that come with the seed. It is most effective to use half-ripened seed as feed. If one puts half-ripened millet or spray millet into the cage, the budgies will leave everything else and feed on that. Planting canary seed is more difficult, as there is a high percentage of empty hulls in the heads.

Budgerigars are capable of raising their young alone when given these foods. It is better, however, to accustom them during the breeding season to a special nesting food. There are different special mixtures commercially available which vary from good to very good. They have only one thing in common: it is difficult to have the budgies accept them, regardless of whether they are in the form of a powder or of a crumbly consistency. It is

*During the breeding and molting seasons, budgies will need extra nutrition in their diets.*

best to introduce nesting foods into aviaries with a breeding colony. To outwit a single breeding pair, one might introduce the food in small quantities, sprinkling it with their favorite sprouted seeds. Particles will cling to the seeds and will be eaten with them. Crumbly mixtures should be mixed with dry seeds so the birds will "accidentally" eat some of it. Once the birds get accustomed to this type of nesting food, one might offer it in special feeding cups. Some birds are absolutely crazy about it as long as their young are small, others will accept only a little of it, and there are those who cannot

be persuaded to try any of it. Strangely enough, there is usually no difference between chicks that have been raised with soft nesting food and those that were raised without it, if they had sufficient other food. Soft food for budgies consists of ground toasted bread or crackers as a base, with dried milk, dried egg, dried shredded insects, honey, and vitamins and minerals added. Some breeders simply use dried bread soaked in milk, adding the above ingredients plus dextrose (sugar), as a soft food. Keets that have become accustomed to it will love it. When fresh it is also easily digestible.

Recently, concentrated vitamins in liquid form, with or without additional protein supplements, have been added to the birds' drinking water and have shown excellent results. These supplements are especially recommended for birds kept in areas where greens and other natural foods are rarely available. They are also good in winter. The only difficulty

*An Australian pied whiteflight cobalt.*

lies in the fact that budgies drink water irregularly and in different quantities. In any case, it is wiser to give your birds more of these concentrated supplements than less. Always follow instructions that come with the supplements. If there are no instructions, it suffices to add a few drops twice a week. Overdoses might be just as harmful as a lack of vitamins. Beware of "miracle drugs" and other remedies that have not been tried out yet by keepers in your area.

Cod-liver oil has so far proven to be the best source of vitamins A and D, especially during seasons of little sunshine; it also serves as a preventive for egg-binding. As it will easily turn dangerously rancid, mix only small quantities with seeds, in proportion to the number of birds to be fed. A recommended mixture is one tablespoon of cod-liver oil to one kg (2.2 pounds) of seeds. It is important to mix it thoroughly so that all seeds become coated with a thin film of the oil. If you use automatic feeding devices, seeds mixed with cod-liver oil

*Greens provide extra nutrition and interest to the budgie's diet. One must, however, take care not to give too much green food.*

will have to be offered in separate cups, as they would olog the feeding device. Budgerigars will accept less oily seed if it is offered in separate feeding cups.

All granivorous birds need small gravel to serve as grindstones in their crops, until the stones themselves become ground up and are absorbed. This is why these birds need a constant supply of sand. As all birds are in need of calcium and minerals to build up their bone structure, feathers and egg shells, a special type of bird grit has been developed, consisting of oyster shell and other natural ingredients. It should be offered to the birds in special feeding cups. There are also special calcium blocks that come in all sizes. Picking on them tends to provide very healthy occupational therapy for keets, and they should be made familiar with these at an early age. Breeding birds should be fed finely powdered calcium, as they will need large quantities of it while laying eggs and raising their young.

*"Ino" is the designation used for red-eyed, pure yellow lutinos and pure white albinos. The yellow bird above is a lutino, while the bird with the mixed green and yellow chest is of an unfixed strain. Tame birds (right) can be sold for a greater price than can untamed birds.*

# Color Strains

All budgerigar color hues, even if they appear very different in color as well as markings to the layman, can be traced back to two basic colors: blue and green. This is why the breeder speaks of green and blue strains from which all other color mutations derive.

To understand this fully, let us first look at the color of the birds known by breeders as the "normal light green" of the wild budgies. Like all other parts of the body, feathers consist of different cells made of a nucleus and the cell membrane. There is a yellow pigment embedded in the membrane. The blue in the feathers of the bird does not represent an organic color, but is caused by an optical effect. When the yellow pigment, which serves as a "yellow-filter," is missing and the distribution of the melanin in the plumage remains the same, the underparts of a bird's body appear blue, but the facial mask appears white. The black and yellow wavy markings of the green birds and the black and white ones of the blue birds are formed by feathers that are evenly alternated, those with a dark color that extends into their external layer and others that are without the dark color. The green birds, however, have the yellow pigment and the blue ones don't. The two long feathers in the middle of the tails of green as well as blue budgies contain so much melanin that yellow pigment—present in green birds—cannot show through. This is why these tail feathers appear to be dark blue in both green and blue birds. Only on very close examination can slight differences in the hue of this blue color be discerned.

To better understand the following explanations of the factors that influence mutations of color and marking in budgerigars, it is necessary to describe the wild green budgie in idealized form. The facial mask from

*A gray green and a normal green budgerigar.*

Above, left to right: Dutch pied clearflight, light green; halfsider recessive pied cobalt; half circular crested normal cobalt. Below, left to right: Australian banded pied normal green; quartersider opaline dark green cobalt; tufted normal skyblue.

Above, left to right: crested normal cobalt; fallow cobalt; fallow light green. Below, left to right: tufted normal dark green; lutino; dark-eyed clear white.

the top of the head to the throat is butter-cup yellow; there are six black spots on the throat, of which the outer ones are partially covered by violet cheek patches on both sides of the head. There is a diagonal wavy pattern from crown to throat, extending to the back and wing-coverts. These markings are black on a yellow background. The underparts, from facial mask downward, are a luminous grass-green, paler in the vent area. The wing-coverts are dull black with green borders. The tail feathers are of graded length, the two longest (in the middle) dark blue, the outer ones dull black and marked with yellow.

A peculiar mixed form, between the blue and green budgies, also exists and is known as a "yellow-faced" budgie. As expressed by the name, yellow is restricted to

*A normal graywing skyblue (left) and a small yellowface skyblue (right).*

*A vocal breeding pair. With the variety of colors found in budgerigar genetics, budgie breeders always look forward to the results each particular mating will bring.*

their facial mask, and the feathers on the side of their tail are also diagonally banded in yellow instead of in white. The basic color—also the color of their underparts—is blue, and the wavy markings are black and white. There are two additional mutations that offset the overall appearance (phenotype). A stronger yellow pigment spreads a delicate yellow veil over all feathers and produces turquoise or bluish turquoise forms. It finally produces individuals that appear in their phenotype practically green, while they belong, according to their genetic make-up (genotype), to the blue color strain.

Although the genetic make-up of yellow-faced birds has not been sufficiently explored to allow a thorough explanation, we know that the pure blue yellow-faced (called mutation I) is produced by a yellow-reducing factor that does not affect any additional

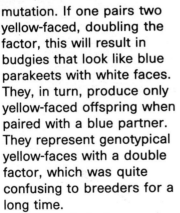

This female is a typically good bird but is not of a "fancy" color variety. The photo below shows a more expensive bird, a lutino. Lutinos must be carefully bred in order to produce lutinos. Lutinos are best mated to dark green to preserve depth of color, and lutino x lutino matings should be avoided. Darker birds are more easily produced.

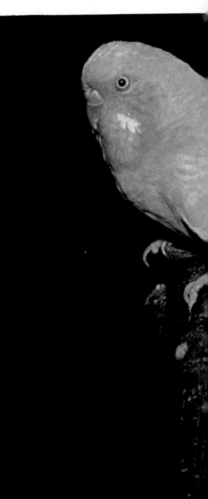

mutation. If one pairs two yellow-faced, doubling the factor, this will result in budgies that look like blue parakeets with white faces. They, in turn, produce only yellow-faced offspring when paired with a blue partner. They represent genotypical yellow-faces with a double factor, which was quite confusing to breeders for a long time.

To conclude, let us say again that all the budgie's colors are regulated by the yellow pigment. Further factors that influence the domesticated budgie's basic color are entirely dependent on feather structure and appear phenotypical to the majority and genotypic to all. We differentiate between the color categories of light, medium and dark. One should remember that light factors do not include any dark factors, medium has one dark factor and dark colors have two. Every breeder may depend upon this very simple law of heredity.

It becomes a little more complicated when green and blue budgies are paired. This is done today by almost all breeders, as the two colors together tend to produce a higher quality of color. We have to talk briefly about the simple concept of heredity in

the animal world, dominant (the controlling or covering genes) and recessive (covered genes) heredity. Green as pure color is always dominant over blue; if one pairs a pure green budgie with a blue one regardless of which sex the green bird is, this will result in green offspring. Their genetic make-up is, however, not pure but "split" for blue. That means that when they are mated among each other they will produce both green and blue.

If one pairs two dark green birds which are made up of two genetically different types, the rules of heredity would slightly differ and the results would be more complicated.

Among the color factors that influence the color of the budgie's plumage are those

An Australian pied normal dark green (left), and a dominant Dutch pied olive green (right).

*A pair of blue-series budgerigars.*

for violet and gray. The way they are influenced is either through different distribution of the melanin or by different forms of the hollow spaces within the feather cells. Violet and gray are dominant hereditary factors and produce very attractive colors. The violet factor can be coupled by the breeder with all others. True violet appears only in birds of the blue series with a dark factor. In other words, cobalts and violets = violet in phenotype. The deepness of the color and its brightness are dependent on the quality of inherited genetics as well as on the pairing of the factors. Violet budgies with a double

*A young wild bird from Australia (left), and a domesticated budgie with similar coloration (below).*

V-factor (V = violet) really should be called lilac. They are very rare, as they are difficult to breed and their shape and size are usually uninteresting. They can be bred only in small numbers by pairing violet with violet. Theoretically this should result in 12.5% lilac, but in reality the percentage is much less, so presumably there is a lethal factor involved. This means that some of the violet chicks with two factors die while in the embryonic stage.

Violet birds with one V-factor vary in the basic color from ultramarine blue to violet blue, and the best ones are a result of selective breeding. Sky blue and the V-factor result in dark blue that is hardly distinguishable from cobalt blue. Mauve and the V-factor result in dark gray-blue offspring with tinted violet feathers. Such birds are classified as violets, sky blues, and violet mauves. Their color genetics again usually follow that of the blue color series. As most violet birds have only one V-factor, this will be transmitted to 50% of their offspring if

one of the breeding pairs carries no V-factor.

If we look at the green series, we will find that the V-factor works genetically in the same way. This is why genotypical violet - green birds are possible and are frequently bred. They are both pretty and valuable, as they will intensify the color when one breeds blue - violet birds. If one pairs, for example, a violet with a green - blue, this will result, according to the above examples, in up to 25% violet - light green. They are quite similar to the dark green birds, but their basic color is much more intense. Violet - dark green birds show an interesting dull darkish green hue; violet - olive birds will be even darker than the usual ones, and often have some violet - mauve feathers on their breast. All cross-breeding from violet-green with blue follows genetically established rules between green and blue, and the V-factor will become dominant for both. There are, however, only about 12.5% true violets obtained from pairing with green birds.

There are two major types of gray or gray-hued parakeets, Australian and English. There was also the slate budgie, which is today virtually extinct. Only the Australian gray is of importance, as their color is dominant. They belong to the blue series and their gray factor is, strangely enough, dominant even over the green wild color. If combined with this color, the result will be gray-green birds. Their color is reminiscent of olive green, but warmer and clearer in its hue; both birds show gray cheek patches and black tail feathers. This will distinguish them even when very young from mauve and olive green birds. Different distributions of melanin and coarser feathers produce the duller but always pure basic color hue that is so distinct that the influence of the three factors (light, medium, and dark) in their phenotype can hardly be seen. Only by cross-breeding gray budgies with those without any gray factor will their genetic existence become visible. For example, light gray with sky blue will produce only gray and sky

*A young gray pied and a violet cock.*

The color of a budgie normally has nothing to do with its value as a pet. The budgie to the left is a yellowwing light green bird of excellent quality. The birds shown below are a normal skyblue and a normal light green with heavy markings on the wing. These wing markings are normal. The yellow-winged bird is a mutation.

blue offspring (proportion 50:50).

If a double gray factor is paired with any partner without gray, it will result in offspring that are exclusively gray or gray-green. These offspring, however, have inherited only one gray factor or carry a split in green or blue. Green and blue offspring that derive from one gray parent cannot be distinguished from each other in their basic colors. This is why they may, without reservation, be used to better a strain, especially the brightness of its color, including violet. As gray and

gray-green budgies are generally very strong and fertile, they are often used for that purpose. One might also be well advised to breed birds with these delicate colors for their color only.

We have now covered all mutations that influence the basic colors of the budgerigar. Now we will talk about those mutations that are expressed by changes in the melanin (dark color factor) in intensity and/or distribution. The scale here reaches from thinning-out or changing of colors to the complete disappearance of the melanin. Some of these forms also show thinning-out or lightening of a basic color, but they are influenced by the same factors. However, all mentioned basic colors will reappear, and they are governed by the same genetic rules.

Graywings have—as expressed in their name—

gray instead of black wings and wavy markings in a hue approximately intermediate between black and white. There are individual differences in both directions on this scale. Their basic color is reduced to approximately halfway between colorless and fully color-reduced, so that one may speak of pastel colors. For example, green will become apple green, blue pastel blue, etc. Nevertheless, the color factors light, medium, and dark are also easily

*Specialized color breeding can create "pastel" colored birds or birds with shockingly bright plumage.*

recognizable in this combination. Graywings are recessive with respect to normal colors. They were once very much in favor, but with the discovery of even more appealing forms, they are seldom bred.

A further lightening of marking and color leads to light yellow (green series) and white sky blues (blue series) with pale gray markings. Breeders refer to these as "ghost-markings," while one could describe their basic colors as yellow and white with a green or blue haze. Nevertheless, with practice the three color hues can be recognized and bred according to established rules. If paired with basic colors, as well as with graywings and clearwings, their genetics are recessive. Before the "inos" were discovered, these colors were thought to be birds that could, by selective breeding, produce yellow and white. Today they are bred for their own qualities and favored as partners for clearwings and inos, as they are usually, in spite of their pastel hues, large and strong birds.

*Headstudy of a budgie. Note the characteristic throat spots.*

Clearwings are among the most favored color strains among specialists. One can distinguish between green yellowwings and blue whitewings. In the best specimens, arrived at by selective breeding, green and blue basic colors are preserved in their regular strength, while the dilution factor influences exclusively color and markings of the back and wings. The most beautiful of the clearwings

No matter what color your pet budgie is, it will enjoy having toys in its cage. Toys are favorable additions to the cage of a budgie who is singly kept. One must remember, however, that the cage should never become too crowded.

*Perches and various playground combinations are fun for budgerigars and will help keep them busy when the owner is away from home.*

will show pale ghost-markings on a yellow or white background. There are, however, all kinds of mutations, some with respect to graywings, others with respect to pastel color, and there is little contrast between basic color and markings. Clearwings tend to be small and unsightly, much like the wild budgie, which is why they are so difficult to breed. Clearwings are recessive to normal colors but dominant to pastel colors that show ghost-markings. This is why they are used to improve the quality of their breed. If they are paired with graywings, a mixed breed results, graywings with bodies full of color as are frequently seen today. The most beautiful are the violet whitewings. To breed them successfully is the ambition of many breeders of special colors. They can be achieved by cross-breeding them with violets of the second generation. All other dark-colored birds are also quite charming, as they show great contrast in color.

Yet another group of colors shows a mutation of

melanin from black to brown in different hues, from pale brown to cinnamon to dark brown. It is interesting that the four browns that are shown today have little in common with each other except for the brown color of their markings, and they are also quite different in their genetic make-up.

During the last few years the cinnamonwings, usually called cinnamons, have become most popular. Their throat spots and wavy markings are cinnamon instead of black, darker in fully colored males than in females. The shafts of their long blue tail feathers are brown with an attractive bluish hue. Cinnamons can be bred in all basic colors, and they are on the average a little paler. The goal is to breed fully cinnamon-colored bodies, which has been achieved by many of the cinnamon lovers. Cinnamons have an especially soft

*A stunning gray male budgerigar.*

plumage but are otherwise robust and fertile parakeets that are frequently used in breeding of other color strains. A specifically charming color can be achieved by crossing violets with cinnamons, the most beautiful specimens thereof showing pinkish violet in their basic coloring. Looking at them closely, one definitely recognizes that the brown factor influences the coloring of their whole plumage.

The genetics of the cinnamon are sex-linked, an expression that is used for the first time here and needs to be explained. Sex-linked characters can only be passed on from the cock bird to his daughters, whereas hens cannot carry sex-linked characters in split form. All of their sons, however, carry the split. This is why one speaks of partial dominance caused by different sex chromosomes in both sexes. Until they are capable of opening their eyes on approximately the sixth day after birth, the eyes of young cinnamons when seen through the skin have a reddish tint that looks brownish later. As soon as they are ready to leave the nest, however, they have gained their normal black color.

Brownwings, which appear only as opalines, are genotypically not different from opaline clearwings. In this combination the markings take on a gray brownish hue. Their basic color can be quite bright.

In very few cases budgies with brown rumps have been reported. There are, however, no exact descriptions or photographs available.

Fallows have deep brown markings, but their basic color is lightened so strongly that all specimens of the green strain superficially appear to be yellow, while all birds of the blue strain appear to be white. Seen close-up, the different color hues caused by different factors can be recognized, especially and most readily on the rump feathers. The genetics of fallows are recessive, and they can theoretically be bred in all known colors. Their eyes, because of a lack of pigment, appear red or plum in varying degrees; the cere of the cock bird is pink to violet instead of blue. Their shape is unfortunately not attractive, which is one of the reasons why they are rarely bred today.

Lacewings came from England. They are yellow and white budgies with weak, light brown, lacy markings on their backs and wings. Lacewings are derived by mutation from the very light inos, and they have the same red eyes. The male's cere is pale pink. Their genetics are sex-linked. Latest test results from test-matings show that they are a combination of inos and cinnamons where strangely enough the cinnamon markings show up again in a weakened form.

"Inos" is a short name for red-eyed pure yellow lutinos and pure white albinos. The lutinos are part of the green series, while the albinos

*An opaline cobalt budgerigar. Opaline budgies have become increasingly popular, as have budgerigars in general.*

represent the blue series. Genetically both are albinos, missing pigment completely, but lutinos have maintained a yellow hue. The most beautiful specimens are egg-yolk yellow, their cheek patches, wings, and tails white; they have red eyes with a whitish sclerotic ring, but their eyes are often very small. There are also pale yellow lutinos with a coarser plumage; these are usually

*No matter what color your pet budgie is, it will be a beautiful, enjoyable addition to your home.*

much stronger birds. Recommended procedure is to pair both of these types resulting in offspring that will be 100% lutinos of both types. Some lutinos, especially the males, show a very pale wavy pattern, while others show a light hue of green on their rumps. Neither of these is desirable when breeding, so the breeder prefers to pair lutino with lutino, which will improve the purity of the color. This can be corrected if one uses normal green or, even better, normal yellow birds, preferably females, as all red-eyed budgies, with the exception of the fallows, are genetically sex-linked. A lutino cock paired with a green female produces a lutino female. A lutino female paired with a green male produces split sex-linked males and genetically pure green females.

While lutinos are favored today, there are fewer good (pure white with red eyes) albinos, though they are of exquisite beauty. Genetic weaknesses, for which the lutinos are well known, appear even more often with albinos, and instead of green they very often show a blue hue on the plumage of their rump, which is not desirable. If one uses gray budgies when breeding albinos, as was done with lutinos by using green and yellow ones, the blue color will disappear and at the same time the albinos will grow larger and more resistant.

All ino cocks have a pinkish violet cere, while that of the female is a normal brownish. Legs and toes of both sexes are flesh-colored; if a budgie is dark, regardless of shade of body color, they are bluish. Their eyes appear to be red as the pigment is missing and the red blood vessels shine through. This is the reason why they are sensitive to light and, if exposed, easily blinded. More than other budgies, they tend to become very excited at night and start raging; they also avoid sunlight. The breeder should be aware of these facts and also take into consideration that these very sensitive birds cannot be raised in outside aviaries in industrial regions. Soot is very hard to remove from

A recessive pied mauve (left), and a pied cobalt green (right).

their plumage, especially as they bathe only in the rain, which in industrial areas is already soiled.

Among all domesticated pets variegated forms are known, and the budgerigar is no exception. In the course of about 100 years three different forms of pied birds were developed. This is a very interesting field, but it tends to become very complicated for the beginner.

Two of those pied forms were developed in Europe; the other was developed in Australia at about the same time and made its way to Europe much later.

Pieds have part of the melanin missing in their plumage, but the places where melanin is missing differ from bird to bird. Only by using virtually identical parents will the offspring be very similar to their parents in markings.

Most easily recognizable of the three forms (and named after the country where they originated) are the recessive Danish pieds, which have some constant markings. They are called harlequins by fanciers and have become very popular. Their wing feathers are yellow or white with dark spots of different sizes distributed in different patterns. These spots also appear at the ends of their wings and on the tips of their tail feathers, which looks rather odd. On their heads and throats frequently appear wavy markings in their small feathers. Their breast is yellow or white, belly and torso green, blue, gray, or violet, and on the flanks and rump you often find light feathers mixed with the others. The most beautiful harlequins show a distinct line of separation between light breast feathers and the dark plumage on their underparts; others show only a long dark spot on the belly and underparts. Females frequently show wavy markings on their backs instead of the usual single dark spots. They might also have completely dark wings and tail feathers. While not especially attractive looking, when paired with a predominantly light male such females might produce very pretty offspring.

One needs a special flair for breeding pieds, but also a lot of plain luck. Strangely enough, in spite of the fact that they are not close in coloring and markings to the wild budgie, the Danish pied tends to be the closest in shape and size to the wild bird. It is narrow and small, with a delicate head, protruding beak, and small spots on the throat. The cheek-patches are violet with white. In health and fertility it also resembles the wild bird.

It is quite difficult to improve the type and size of pieds, as to do so successfully would require cross-breeding with much larger and heavier birds of darker color. As Danish pieds are recessive, pieds would be expected only in the second generation of such a cross. It is necessary to keep exact notes and band all birds, and single breeding cages have to

*An Australian dominant pied opaline gray green (left), and an Australian banded pied yellowface cobalt (right).*

be used.

The most prominent markings of recessive Danish pieds are pure black eyes without the white sclerotic ring. The male shows a pale pink cere, as do the inos. Both male and female show light legs as well as light toes.

Dominant Dutch pieds are distinguished from Danish pieds most prominently by the normal color of their eyes and ceres. They also have a yellow (white in the blue series) spot approximately the size of a thumb nail on the nape, and the light mask usually extends to the breast, forming a kind of apron. They show a series of dark spots on the throat. The darkest specimens do not show any lightening of color. The lightest colored birds might be spotted in an irregular pattern all over their bodies, so that they resemble the harlequin. Dutch pieds are usually of better size and form than harlequins. Their colors, however, often run, so that they look somewhat washed out. As they are dominant they are easier to breed in large numbers, so the breeder has enough to select from for further cross-breeding.

By selection, clearflights were bred from Dutch pieds. They should show exclusively light wings and tail feathers, but no other yellow or white feathers except for their nape spot and light throat. Breeders used to eagerly breed clearflights, but unfortunately this has declined. It is especially regrettable as a well-marked clearflight is something to behold. However, it is not possible to breed this series directly. Even if a pair of the best clearflights were mated their offspring would not necessarily be clearflights.

Also dominant are the Australian pieds, which show many positive traits of the Danish and Dutch pieds in their phenotype, although

they are not genetically close. The Australian is the most desired of color series among the pieds, as its markings are the best defined and most appealing. They share with the Dutch pieds their light nape spot, but the mask on the throat remains normal in size. The wing and tail feathers are light from the bend downward, but in differing widths of lightness from a small light line to completely light wing covers; the most beautiful birds have pure yellow or white wings. The body color ranges from very dark to an almost completely light breast and underparts with all color shades. Some show only a green or blue band a few centimeters wide over the breast, while others have a uniform light band on a dark base that extends approximately around the middle of their bodies. The latter are the most desired type, the banded pieds, but they are very difficult to breed as it is hard to genetically fix their markings, just as it is with clearflights. The distribution of light and dark on top of the body is also varied. A symmetrical distribution is desired and possible to a degree, but the results are often quite asymmetrically marked birds, such as those with: one light and one dark wing; one white and one violet cheek spot; regularly distributed cheek spots on one side and a cheek band without spots on the other; completely or partially missing throat spots; and light breast markings that look like a cross. If one pairs two very good banded pieds, it will result in offspring that are too lightly colored. Breeders therefore use one non-pied bird with a pied partner; it is unimportant which of the two is male or female. As they are dominant, one can expect up to 50% pieds, of which, however, hardly one is the same as the other. Every pied is attractive on its own, so even asymmetrical birds find admirers. Whether markings that can be inherited in a constant form will be bred in the future, as has happened in pigeons, remains to be seen. After all, domesticated budgerigars are still young as a race.

An excellent example of an opaline cobalt.

Opaline budgies are now strongly influencing all other colors. Their name refers to the semiprecious opal that shimmers with bluish green hues; the wing-coverts of the most attractive specimens of this variety have the same blue-green gleam. The gleam is caused by a different blue structure of their feathers. More important for the individuality of the opaline is the distribution of the melanin, which is quite different from that of the wavy markings of wild birds and does not depend on being black, of diluted color, or brown. This is why there are opalines in all color groupings and showing all colors. The body color is distributed all over the plumage, much as in normally marked budgies. The top of the head of a green opaline, for example, is yellowish green and the back is green with or without black or brown spots. The wings show spotted rather than wavy markings, while every dark wing covert shows a wide green stripe instead of a narrow yellow one, as is the case with all normal wavy patterns. This produces a striking effect loved by many of the fanciers of the opalines. The basic color in some of the birds surpasses even the normal colors in depth and intensity, but there are also specimens with washed-out colors. It is difficult for the breeder to achieve a bird with a uniformly colored back free of black spots or to remove ugly pale tail feathers. Opalines are robust, fertile birds that are sex-linked, only partially dominant, and produce enough material for selective breeding. Opalines are also being used to improve

degenerated normal strains or to breed special characteristics such as round throat spots, for which they are genetically predestined.

There are three different opaline factors that only differ slightly in how they affect mutations. If one wants to breed pure, bright colors, especially uniformly colored plumage on the back, select those birds that show these qualities. Also, pair spotted birds, or those with washed-out colors, with normally marked ones. Their offspring would then show more black spots on the back, but their basic colors would be of a greater intensity. Negative qualities of the opalines are impure coloring on the forehead and a mask that is too small. These qualities are easily inherited, and the breeder should watch out for them, as no one likes such birds.

Half-siders occasionally create a sensation at a show. They are budgies with one half of the body colored blue, the other half green. Their coloring is sometimes arranged symmetrically, sometimes asymmetrically.

A normal violet budgerigar. Always remember to plan all matings carefully, as preparedness will help reduce the incidence of defective offspring.

Breeders have for many years tried to breed these birds, but without success, as this peculiar coloring does not represent a mutation, but rather a genetic accident that occurs when cells are split while still in an embryonic state of development. This is the reason why only a tendency can be inherited, if at all, and half-siders are, for obvious reasons, often weak and have poor fertility.

# Color Combinations

Theoretically it is possible to combine all of the budgerigar color characters with each other, which would result in a wide variety of colors and shapes. To mention all of those and breeding combinations would go far beyond the reach of this book. Additionally, some combinations are hardly an improvement in color over the parents and would result in little interest from practical breeders. We will mention only the more attractive and important combinations

With the help of yellow-faced factors, which are dominant, you can produce in one generation lemon-yellow inos (yellow-faced and albinos) and three colored pieds (yellow-white-blue) if dominant pieds (Dutch pieds or Australian pieds) are used. If recessive pieds are used, the results will show in the second generation. Combining yellow-faced factors and opaline with whitewing cobalts or, even better, whitewing violets results after a few generations in a budgie that shows all the colors of the rainbow and is actually called a rainbow budgie. Because there is an accumulation of combined factors, it is impossible to breed these birds as a pure variety, since the factors will split again into their original colors. This is the reason why rainbows are seldom seen. Similar birds of delicate pastel-color mixtures can be produced with the help of the cinnamon factor.

From the combinations of graywings, clearwings, and opalines in only a few generations can be produced almost unicolored delicate green or blue budgies, the selfs. These can be reproduced in their pure form, provided care is taken to breed them selectively according to their basic genetic make-up. There would be more of these birds if there were more budgie lovers who would breed them in a more scientific way.

For some years cinnamon opalines have been very much in vogue in all known basic colors. They are relatively easy to breed, as both types are sex-linked. An opaline male paired with a cinnamon female produces offspring that are split in cinnamon as well as opaline. A cinnamon female mated with an opaline male produces cinnamon opaline females and cinnamon/opaline males, which then reproduce cinnamon opaline in both sexes. Breeding pieds with birds of weakened or otherwise changed color characters (for example graywings, clearwings, yellow-greens, fallows, etc.) is not recommended, while cinnamon pieds and opaline pieds may turn out especially beautiful and are very much liked. Choosing dominant pieds (the Australian and

*Before breeding a particular bird, be sure that it is healthy and in excellent condition.*

Dutch pieds) and also good opalines, cinnamons, and cinnamon opalines to produce the pied effect will produce good results within one or two generations. Recessive Danish pieds are not suitable for combinations because good results take much longer and are very often not recognizable externally.

The same is true for the combination of different pied varieties. There is one exception to this that has confused breeders for quite a while. Quite by chance it was discovered that Dutch pieds crossed with Danish pieds may under certain circumstances produce pure yellow and pure white budgies with black eyes and without the light sclerotic ring. The male shows a pinkish violet instead of blue cere, and both male and female have light flesh-colored legs. They therefore resemble, in part, Danish pieds and inos. Genotypically they are Danish Dutch pieds, in which combination due to a coupling of specific factors the melanin, except in the eyes, disappears. Dutch

pieds crossed with Danish pieds produce, regardless of sex, Dutch pieds split Danish pieds. If one cross-breeds these among themselves, they produce in the next generation approximately 25% yellow or white blackeyes (yellow from the green series, white from the blue). These blackeyes, cross-bred among themselves or back to their parental forms, result in pieds in both their forms, in blackeyes, and, under certain circumstances, also in non-pied budgies. But if one pairs blackeyes with blackeyes, the result is some blackeyes that are pure in their genetic make-up, as the pertinent characters have been doubled, but they are only recognizable in test-matings. If you have some and are able to recognize them, breeding them to each other results in 100% pure color, so that you may have a series of pure yellow and pure white budgies that are not albinos.

Albinos and lutinos can be combined with all other colors as their genetic characters "represent" every other color, depending on the forms from which they were bred. In phenotype these colors are covered by albino characteristics, but they recur when paired with dark birds. The covered basic color is in some cases discernible in the bird's phenotype. This is why lutinos covering gray green appear to be mustard yellow and albinos that cover cinnamon violet might appear to have a pinkish hue.

This one raised hopes for red budgies but it is not possible to breed them, as the color character red is not contained in the budgie plumage. Red also cannot be achieved by cross-breeding with the much larger grass parakeets *(Neophema)* that have red colors—the few hybrids produced are sterile, presuming you can make a budgie mate with a grass parakeet to begin with. Don't be deceived by red budgerigars that have been color-fed with dyes.

Also, attempts to breed black parakeets from mauves, grays, and slate grays have not resulted in more than dark slate gray birds. There have been

A normal cinnamon graywing budgerigar.

relatively few attempts made at this combination, as the invariably dull gray transitional forms would find few buyers.

If one looks at the sometimes bizarre forms caused by mutation of plumage characters in chickens, pigeons, and canaries, changes in the form of the budgerigar seem modest in comparison. Crested budgies were produced in Canada and China beginning in the thirties and are still bred today; England even has a special club for crested budgie breeders. Three different kinds of crested budgies are known today: tufted, half-crested, and full-crested, of which the full-crested is the most popular. As far as is known, all types of crests are governed by the same factor, which is dominant and doubled with a 48% lethality in the embryonic state. This is unfortunately the case in all domesticated crested birds, so that a crested bird is, as a rule, paired with a non-crested one. Because of this, consistently crested budgies cannot be produced, as crested birds with only one factor are very variable. Some have only crests of small raised feathers that seem out of proportion on the budgie's head. The best crests look somewhat like caps and are on half-crested birds. Feather crests are formed by a swirl at the root of the feathers, forcing the feather to grow upward and sideways instead of in layers as in normal plumage. Double-crested budgies are, regrettably, usually not fertile and tend to have abnormal behavior problems due to disorders in their nervous system. They are hardly for the beginning breeder and seem to appeal to only a limited number of people anyway. A separated double-swirl crest is also known.

As far as known, feather-legs (birds with little feather on one or both legs) are very rarely seen and, in spite of systematic breeding experiments, have not been genetically fixed. One must presume that the experiments were not continued with the necessary persistence because practical knowledge gained from pigeons would lead one to believe that feather-legs will reappear.

Recently, in domestic Australian, British, and

German birds, quite independently of each other, some individual birds were bred that by far exceeded all known conventional mutations. Their down plumage grew sparsely but up to 12 cm (5 inches) long, so that the normal outlines of a budgie were not recognizable anymore in published photographs. The throat spots, which are on one feather, hung down to the floor, and the body feathers grew in a twisted manner, probably caused by several swirls. Wing and tail feathers were normal with some of the birds, degenerate in others; these birds were unable to fly. Some died early, but others seemed quite healthy. It is not known if they have ever been mated, although for purely technical reasons this seems improbable. While the Australians poetically dubbed this aberration "chrysanthemums," the English named them, more appropriately, "feather-dusters."

Color and markings of these birds were washed out, but they at least showed what kind of surprises a budgie is capable of producing.

*A normal light green budgie. Breeders may occasionally produce interesting non-color mutations, but most of these traits are difficult to fix in type.*

# The Pet Budgerigar

As recently as the 1920s it was believed that a budgie kept alone would die of loneliness. Although this can really happen if an older bird used to other budgies is suddenly deprived of their company, it is very uncommon. It is important to start out with a young budgie if you want to tame it, and only a very tame bird will imitate the human voice and other sounds. It has been shown that birds approximately three weeks old can be taken from the nest box and raised quite successfully on warm mush prepared from hulled millet, grit, and oats with added vitamins and minerals. Birds that have been raised this way will become exceptionally tame and attached to their keepers and will become as strong and healthy as birds raised by their own mothers. If taken very early from the nest boxes, they will not have developed their instinct to escape, and their human keeper will within a few days be accepted as surrogate mother. In this way the young budgie will be patterned to human sounds, which come quite naturally to a young budgie. A budgerigar is hatched with only those innate sounds that will remain with him all his life. Everything else is strictly learned. It is, however, quite time-consuming to raise such a sparsely feathered bird baby with its undershot beak, as for three weeks it will have to be fed every three hours with freshly prepared and warmed mush, first with an eye-dropper and later with a small spoon. If you are not a breeder yourself, it will also be difficult to obtain such nestlings. In view of the risk involved, few breeders are inclined to part with such young chicks unless they know the person very well and are convinced that he has the necessary experience to raise such a young bird.

It was also discovered that naturally raised, independent young birds kept in isolation from the beginning of the fifth and not later than the tenth week develop into equally lovable pets if they have been treated in the right way from the beginning. The younger the bird is, the easier this can

Wild budgerigars live in large flocks; it is therefore important that the owner of the pet budgie have enough time to spend with a singly kept bird.

*Two or more budgies kept together will bond to each other rather than to their owner, but they will keep each other happily occupied.*

be accomplished; if the bird is a little older, it takes some patience. There are many respectable commercial breeders that offer such young birds, and the technical term "nestling" that they use expresses the fact that they have been taken out of their nest only recently. You may recognize these young birds from their relatively large dark eyes that have not developed a light sclerotic ring yet, and by their wavy head markings that extend in dark budgies to the root of the beak.

The new acquisition should be taken home as quickly as possible, and a cage should be ready. There are a large variety of cages available commercially, so you can choose one according to your taste and pocketbook. You may find every design from the traditional cage to something that almost looks like it was designed by Picasso. The latter might well cater to the modern tastes of their owners, but not to the comfort of the birds that will be housed there for many years. The best cages are rectangular ones with bottom trays removable for easy cleaning. There should be a latching door on either side of the cage or the roof. Take care that the door is not the type that closes in such a way that it could act as a guillotine.

*A pair of young budgerigars. The younger the budgie is when acquired, the easier it will be to tame. It must not, however, be removed from the nest too soon.*

*A pair of normal skyblue yellowfaces, mother and son.*

Don't crowd the cage with too many gadgets, and be sure the bird has plenty of room. You could outfit the cage with a tree for climbing, a small ladder, and one or two perches. Swings and toys hanging from strings could cause accidents. Plastic toys

*Perches are an extremely important furnishing for the budgie cage, as their use will prevent claws from growing too long and damaging the foot.*

are recommended for birds left alone a lot. Seed cups may be open or with a partial lid, but there have been inexperienced birds that died of hunger because they could not locate the food in partially closed seed cups. Breeders do not use this type of seed cup, as the budgie usually does not dirty his seed. In any case, leave some seed on the floor of the cage, at least in the beginning, and fasten some millet sprays to the cage bars. When first put alone into a cage, the young keet needs seed right in front of his eyes or he will forget to eat.

For the first two weeks, speak to the bird in a friendly tone of voice, avoid quick movements, and otherwise leave him alone. He will, according to his temperament, sit sadly on his perch or restlessly fly around in his cage, twisting and twitching. These are signs the bird is very unhappy, wants to return to his own kind, and is afraid of being alone. He climbs around because of a displacement complex that helps him to calm his fears and reduces his urge to

escape. This behavior is quite normal.

We mentioned that during all seasons budgerigars spend their life in close social contact with each other. Naturally a captive bird becomes very disturbed when the normal rhythm of his life is suddenly interrupted and he is taken into new surroundings. This fact, however, accounts for his ability to become so closely attached to his keeper. Once he has formed this attachment, his human keeper will be everything for him; friend, one of his kind, even sex partner, which might at times be a little embarrassing but should be taken with humor. Budgies patterned this way will be unable to respond if given the company of another bird or a mate after years of having been alone. After having been alone for two years, they cannot be used for breeding anymore.

The first captive response a young bird shows is a quick opening and closing of the eyes when his keeper walks up to his cage and talks to him. Soon he will come to the cage bars, at which time one should carefully extend an open hand toward him. Only when he has learned to trust your fingers and starts playing with your hand, climbing around on it inside his cage, might you carefully take him out of the cage. Once he trusts you, he will regard you as a tree to climb around in and provide a resting place, and he will return to you even after making the first scouting flight around the room. Should he get scared into shooting up to your curtain rod, it is best to leave him there until he gets hungry.

*Budgies, by their nature, will climb to the highest possible perch they can find.*

Offer him his full seed cup on your out-stretched hand. A few minutes later you will be ready to take your eagerly feeding bird on your hand and return him to his cage. The first lesson has now been successfully completed and should be repeated daily.

Soon, when you open his cage your bird will fly toward you, hop around, and explore everything. When he is hungry he will return to his cage. Some keets will let themselves be easily returned to their cage perched on your finger if you trick them with a

*If pet budgies are given a healthy diet and a clean environment, they can live as long as twelve to fifteen years.*

*A lutino budgerigar.*

special treat. By trying to chase or grab a young keet, even with the help of towels or a broom, you will exasperate your bird. If necessary, wait until dark and then, with a sure grip, take him from his roosting place.

The young keet needs a lot of sleep and likes to snooze a little during the day. If you stay up late at night and the bird cage is in the same room, cover it up.

To teach your bird to talk, you will have to wait until he is completely tame and attached to you. The best time for lessons is twilight. A woman's voice is best. Start with two or three words, repeated over and over. First teach him his name and then his address; quite a few lost birds have been returned home this way. Short words with many vowels are easiest to learn. Some birds will easily imitate their first words after a few weeks, but others may take up to half a year, so continue teaching for that period of time. Not every bird will learn to talk, but the reason for this is more often the teacher than the bird.

Male birds as a rule learn more and better than females, because the males have a wider range of sounds. They easily learn to laugh, whistle, imitate banging of doors, other bird calls, and even songs. But even if you have a bird that is not that gifted, you will love him.

Budgies reach maturity between the sixth and the ninth months, at which time they will display some courting behavior. A courting male regurgitates his food, as though feeding his mate. Although not exactly esthetic, this is not an illness, as many people fear. He will also show other signs of displacement behavior, but these soon pass, as budgies reach their peak readiness for breeding only occasionally. The behavior of pet birds might seem a little annoying during this time, but some of it can be avoided by removing the mirror, which provides stimulation. Also avoid stimulating foods such as eggs, meat, sugar, and cake. While eating, your bird belongs in his cage.

*An Australian pied cobalt. The newly acquired budgie must be given time to adjust to his new home.*

# The Sick Budgerigar

"An ounce of prevention is better than a pound of cure" is a time-worn phrase that this chapter wants to promote. To cure and save is not always possible, especially when an illness has been recognized too late. A sick budgie will sit listlessly in his cage with dull eyes. When its illness gets worse, the budgie hides its head in its plumage as though sleeping, but rests on both legs instead of one as the healthy bird will do. There may be a watery nasal discharge. Seeds are either hulled and not eaten cr just ignored. These symptoms indicate either a cold caused by a draft and/or dampness or an inflammation of the digestive system which might have been caused by spoiled food. The bird will have to be isolated immediately and kept in a warm place. Instead of water, give it weak tea, millet seeds, and oats. Stop feeding all greens and juicy fruits. In most mild cases this will be sufficient treatment. Should the bird not improve within a day or two, transfer it to a hospital cage. Any single cage will do when equipped with an infrared lamp placed in front of the cage in such a manner that the bird might seek out its warmth but may also retreat from it. Test with your hand how far from the cage the lamp has to be placed so it will not be too warm.

Many medications for common diseases of budgies are available at your pet shop, so check there for anything that is obviously minor. If in doubt, go to a good vet immediately. Birds have a high metabolism and will not survive long if they stop feeding and drinking.

For some years budgie breeders have been plagued by contagious crop diseases. The bird brings up a sticky mucus that will soon soil the bird's head plumage. It sits with closed eyes and will die if help is not immediately at hand. A drop of tetracycline put undiluted into the beak will result in recovery the very next day. If a bird is not treated, however, it will just as quickly die.

A word about egg-binding is necessary, although it rarely occurs if the bird is regularly given cod-liver oil

*A violet male and a green pied male.*

and vitamins. This condition requires immediate attention. The female sits on the floor of the cage, repeatedly strains to pass the egg as long as she is still strong enough, and whips her tail up and down. She should be placed in a warm hospital cage or under an infrared lamp, and a little oil should be smeared around the vent. Usually half an hour later the egg will be laid, and the bird is her old self again. She will not continue to lay, however, and should have some rest. This condition is especially dangerous when it happens to older females that have been kept alone most of the time. Even if they have never laid eggs before, they might still develop the urge after four or five years, perhaps from being fed stimulating foods from human table scraps. The only real remedy is prevention by giving your bird natural, healthy food. An older female's pelvis does not stretch sufficiently to allow an egg to pass. A veterinarian or a trained layman might succeed in crushing the egg, so that it may be passed in pieces, but the smallest injury will lead to infection and death.

For some decades a lot has been written about French Molt and a lot of research has been done without finding an exact solution. This is not actually an illness, but is really a deficiency. It probably can be traced directly to the feeding of the chicks in the nesting box. The crop-milk prepared by the parent bird probably lacks some substance, perhaps protein. The chicks need this for the growth of their plumage, and a lack of it will cause most of their wing feathers to fall out shortly before they harden, approximately at the time of their leaving the nest box. This definitely was first observed by French breeders, which is where the name comes from. Young birds with this deficiency run around on the floor, incapable of flying, so they have been called "runners." Some of their feathers might grow in at a later time, others never. French Molt was once quite disturbing to many a breeder, as chicks that are afflicted are not exactly pretty. Today the problem is greatly reduced if the birds are fed protein, trace elements, and vitamin supplements. Experiences with these remedies, which are simply added to the birds' drinking water, are mixed, but many breeders have had excellent results. French Molt has almost disappeared, and fertility has been significantly improved.

Simple broken limbs heal best when left alone, and complicated ones are usually hopeless, as the budgie will sooner or later remove any splint or bandage with his beak and not allow the broken limb to heal.

# Index

Albino, 92
Australian pied, 100
Aviaries, 36, 38, 41
Banding, 22, 23, 52, 53
Bathing, 21, 32
Beak trimming, 32
Breeding cages, 44–47
Brownwing, 92
Cages, 112
Cere, 50
Cinnamon, 88
Classification, 7
Claw trimming, 32
Clearwing, 85
Colony breeding, 38, 40
Color mutations, 68–107
Courting, 32, 47
Crested, 108
Crop milk, 49
Danish pied, 98
Dutch pied, 99
Egg-binding, 122
Egg-laying, 48
Fallow, 92
Feather duster, 109
Feather leg, 108
Feather plucking, 52, 54, 55
Fostering, 49
French molt, 124
Genotype, 73

Germination, 59, 62
Gray, 80
Graywing, 83
Green food, 60
Half-sider, 102
Interrupting breeding, 50
Lacewing, 92
Lighting, 38
Lutino, 92
Mauve, 79
Nest boxes, 38–45
Nesting food, 62, 63
Opaline, 101
Pastel, 84
Perches, 46
Phenotype, 73
Pied, 97
Poisonous plants, 28
Preening, 28
Sand, 65
Sex linked characters, 91
Spray millet, 62
Talking, 120
Toys, 114
Violet, 77
Vitamins, 64
Water, 32
Wild green, 68
Yellowface, 72

PAISLEY & DISTRICT BUDGERIGAR SOCIETY SPECIAL AWARD

BUDGERIGA... ... nd BEST BEGINNER /65

E. N. Hillier & Sons Ltd., Printers, Bus...

**BUDGERIGARS**
KW-011